How To Make Some Money While Helping Save The Planet

Re - Think Your Recycling - For Cash!

Frank Palaia

CONTENTS

WHY RECYCLE?

Why are we doing this?   There may be more reasons to recycle than you might think.

Make some money

"Saving the planet" sure sounds great, but there are bills to pay.   You may need gas for the car – you may need to buy groceries! This book will give you some real-world examples of ways that you can make some money recycling. You could turn some of the ideas in this book into a way to make a living, but for most people, it's only going to be a way to make a little extra money from time to time.

The availability and profitability of the recycling opportunities listed in this book will vary depending on your location, and current market conditions. Additionally, it's important to follow local recycling guidelines and regulations to ensure that materials are recycled properly.

Save the planet

So – can we really save the planet? Let's hope so. There are piles of plastic floating to islands in the south pacific. Plastic debris is carried over long distances from various sources to remote islands by ocean currents, including the South Equatorial Current and the East Australian Current. Plastic waste also ends up in the ocean through illegal dumping or inadequate waste infrastructure.

Abandoned or lost fishing gear, such as nets and buoys, can contribute to plastic pollution. The South Pacific is a region with significant fishing activities, and abandoned gear washes ashore on islands.

Larger plastic items can break down over time into smaller particles known as microplastics. These microplastics can be transported over long distances by ocean currents and may accumulate on remote islands.

Efforts to address plastic pollution in the South Pacific often involve a combination of local waste management improvements, community education, and international cooperation to reduce plastic production and improve waste disposal practices. Initiatives like beach clean-ups, recycling programs, and awareness campaigns are crucial in mitigating the impact of plastic pollution on these islands. International agreements and collaborations are also essential to address the issue at its source and reduce the overall production and distribution of single-use plastics.

We can all contribute to the solution, by doing whatever we can to recycle not only plastics, but other materials.

Young recyclers can learn some valuable skills and life lessons. You might be surprised at the entrepreneurial skills that can be developed with a little recycling business. It can require patience, and delivering at a scrap yard or recycling center can present an opportunity for young recyclers to develop their negotiating skills.

SELLING ON EBAY

You might be saying, "I thought this was a book about recycling?". It is – but recycling isn't just about collecting cardboard or scrap metal, and taking it to a scrap yard or a municipal recycling center, or transfer station. There are arguments regarding who first came up with the "reduce, reuse, recycle" slogan, but selling on ebay fits right into it.

Why throw something away that will end up in a land fill (or worse – as pollution somewhere), when you can sell it on ebay to someone who can use it again? It's a win-win. It's actually a triple win, because you get to make some money, someone else gets to purchase something they want or need, and the planet wins, because an item that might have otherwise ended up in a trash heap gets an extended life.

An entire book could be written about making money by selling things on ebay – and in fact – there are many books on this topic already available. Lots of them are even free – so check some out. Meanwhile, here are some key points to keep in mind.

Look for items that are small, not fragile, and light weight. Why? – because you will need to be able to ship them - sometimes to God-forsaken places - and you want to do that while keeping the cost low, so keep the item size and the weight down. "Not fragile" is important, because if you sell something breakable there's a good chance that it won't make it to the buyer, and then you'll have the hassle of a refund – or worse – a buyer could tell you that the item arrived broken, and you'll have no way of knowing if they're telling you the truth unless you insist that they return it first, which only presents additional cost and a second opportunity for a fragile item to be broken again.

If you sell a fragile item to someone on ebay, and they contact you to tell you it arrived damaged (or that it is not as you described it), minimize your losses. Apologize, give them a full refund immediately, and tell them they can keep the item. Do this to maintain a good standing on ebay. You only want good reviews. A bad review will send your potential buyers looking for another seller.

If you have a valuable, but fragile item that is worth money, you can still sell it, but don't use ebay. Sell it locally, at a pawn shop, or on facebook marketplace. When you use facebook marketplace, there is no seller's fee, and you can arrange for local pickup. You can meet buyers in front of your garage, or at a coffee shop, and fragile items can be handled with care.

When you have a particularly large, valuable item that you'd like to sell, ebay is usually out. (There are some exceptions, such as for automobiles and motorcycles). Shipping large items becomes too difficult or prohibitively expensive. This is another time to go with facebook marketplace, or Craig's list. You'll be meeting your buyers in-person for local pick-up.

When meeting buyers to sell something for local-pick-up, keep your personal safety in mind. Don't invite people that you don't know inside your home. Meet them outdoors or in a public place.

If you can, get paid, or get a deposit first, because there are a lot of time-wasters out there. These are people who will tell you that they are going to show up, who won't. Or - they may keep you waiting somewhere. You can ask them to send you money up front, using Venmo or PayPal. This way, you'll know that they're serious.

If getting the cash up front does not seem reasonable – perhaps a buyer may need to inspect an item first - you can still prevent prospective buyers from wasting your time. If you have a valuable item, tell them, "cash only, and first-come, first-serve". Don't ever agree to "hold" something for someone unless they've given you a deposit, as they may not be a serious buyer who will show up. Tell them, "whomever shows up with the cash first" gets your item. If they want what you have to sell, they'll get moving.

Most people are honest. You could get burned doing this, but if you have an item that requires local pick-up that isn't worth a fortune, you can make it a little easier on yourself. If you live in a neighborhood where it will work, you can leave an item on your porch for a buyer, and tell them that they can come and pick it up whenever they'd like, and that they can leave the money for you under the door mat. Sure, you could get robbed, but more often than not, the item will get collected and your money will be there. This way, you don't have to interrupt your day to meet someone, or get involved in a lengthy conversation with someone you'll probably never see again. This is a great approach if you're selling an item that you would have just thrown away anyway. What have you got to lose?

One final thought - about on-line scammers. There are so many of them! It's not so much a concern when you're selling on ebay, but when you're selling on facebook marketplace or Craig's list, you will very likely run into someone who will try to take advantage of you. Watch for the instant messages that don't quite read well. English may be the sender's second language. If someone asks for your cell phone number so that they can talk about the item that you're selling – it's usually a red flag! Scammers need valid cell phone numbers so that they can set up free gmail accounts. Cell phone numbers are used for account verification. They'll use your number and then come up with some ridiculous excuse as to why they need you to share a code that has been sent to your phone. Don't fall for this. If a discussion needs to be had regarding the item you're selling, try and stick with the messaging tool on the platform, or offer to call them – and get them to give you their phone number, instead of giving them yours.

Also – don't accept checks. Another scam; "I'll send you a check, and then I'll have my son come pick up the item." Red flag! You could hand over the item without ever being able to identify the "buyer", and then the check will bounce. Accept cash only.

SHOW ME THE MONEY

Let's get down to it. Here are things that you can recycle for money.

Return beverage cans and bottles for the deposit.

If your state has a bottle return program, you'll get a nickel per bottle. A few states will pay 10 cents per bottle. Some states require that each bottle be loaded into a machine, which spins it and reads a bar code, before crushing or shredding it. This means you can't crush them ahead of time so that they take up less space. If you're saving a lot of bottles, some of them can get sticky, so you need to spend time washing out each bottle before storage, or be prepared for a bit of a sticky mess. It's not likely that you'll be able to save up for your retirement doing this, but it's a great way to teach kids about recycling, encourage young entrepreneurship, or teach them about saving up their own money for ice cream.

As of January 2022, here is a list of states with a bottle recycling program, and their payment per bottle. If you live just over the border in a neighboring state, you can probably still collect bottles.

California:

5 cents for containers less than 24 ounces and 10 cents for containers 24 ounces or larger

Connecticut:	5 cents
Delaware:	5 cents
Hawaii:	5 cents
Iowa:	5 cents
Maine:	5 cents
Massachusetts:	5 cents
Michigan:	10 cents
New York:	5 cents
Oregon:	10 cents
Vermont:	5 cents

Car Parts:

Aluminum wheels and head gaskets are worth money. Catalytic converters contain a number of precious metals that are worth money at the scrap yard. When selling car parts at the scrap yard, here are some things to keep in mind:

Before heading to the scrap yard, sort and separate the different types of car parts. This makes it easier for the yard to process and weigh each type individually, potentially leading to higher payouts.

Strip the parts of any non-metal components like plastic, rubber, or glass. This enhances the value of the metal and ensures that the scrap yard classifies the parts correctly.

Some car parts may contain high-value metals like aluminum, copper, or stainless steel. Identify and separate these parts, as they will fetch a higher price than regular steel.

Different scrap yards may have specific requirements for accepting car parts. Before bringing your parts to a yard, check their guidelines regarding acceptable materials, preparation, and any other specific requirements.

Here are some specific car parts that are worth you're trouble to scrap:

Catalytic converters contain precious metals like platinum, palladium, and rhodium. They can be among the most valuable car parts at a scrap yard, but not all scrap yards pay the same amounts for them. Also, some catalytic converters are worth much more than others. In Rhode Island, at the time of publication, we can get "between $5 and $50, depending on the make and model", according to the woman who works at the scale house at the local scrap yard. If you can find a yard that specializes in catalytic converters, you can get more.

Because catalytic converters can be so valuable, theft is a problem. In some cities, thieves will slip under a parked car with a cutting wheel to steal catalytic converters. Now many scrap yards are requiring that you provide a copy of the vehicle registration from which the catalytic converter originated, to deter theft. Make sure you have it so that you don't get stuck.

Aluminum wheels are lightweight and valuable. They are usually worth more than steel wheels due to the higher market value of aluminum.

Some high-end or performance vehicles have stainless steel exhaust systems, which can be more valuable than regular steel.

Radiators are typically made of aluminum or aluminum-copper, both of which have scrap value.

Transmissions can contain various metals, including aluminum and steel. The overall weight contributes to their scrap value.

Engine blocks are often made of cast iron or aluminum. The material composition affects their value at a scrap yard.

Vehicles contain copper wiring in various components of the electrical system. Copper has a high scrap value.

Brake calipers are often made of aluminum or a combination of aluminum and steel, making them valuable at scrap yards.

Alternators and starters contain copper wiring and may have other valuable metals, contributing to their scrap worth.

Scrap metal

Collect scrap metal, such as copper, brass, aluminum, steel, red brass, and lead. Sell it to scrap yards. Prices will vary based on the metal type and market demand. If your state does not have a bottle return program, you can include your aluminum cans in your scrap metal collection.

You don't want to mix the scrap metal that you collect in a giant heap. It will have to be sorted so that you can get the most per pound for it, so it's easier to sort it as you collect it. An easy way to start is to sort the smaller pieces into five-gallon buckets, for each type of scrap metal. You can put them in the corner of your basement and take your time collecting. If you're only tossing something into your buckets from time to time, it might take you a few years to get enough saved to make it worth a trip to the scrap metal yard – but imagine how fun it will be to load your buckets into a truck one day, and drive home with between $200 - $300.

Pictured above; some aluminum poles, some copper pipes, and buckets loaded with sorted scrap metal, ready for a trip to the scrap metal yard.

PAYMENT RECEIPT

Exeter Scrap Metal
405 Nooseneck Hill Road
Exeter, RI 02898
401-397-2727

ConnecticutScrap.com

Receipt: 224464

Customer: ESM22620

Date: 12/10/2022

Time: 11:02:49 AM

Ticket: 223346

Operator: ESM K

Weigh In: 12/10/2022 10:50:54 AM

Weigh Out: 12/10/2022 11:02:30 AM

All weights are in pounds unless otherwise noted

Commodity	Gross	Tare	Net	Price	TOTAL $
Alum OldSheet	63	4	59	0.4000/LB	24.00
Comp/Red Brass	30	2	28	2.0500/LB	57.00
#1 Copper	48	8	40	3.0500/LB	122.00
Brass	9	2	7	1.4500/LB	10.00
Dirty Brass	20	3	17	0.7000/LB	12.00
				Ticket Total:	225.00

No. of Tickets: 1

Payment Method: EZCash

Total Paid: $225.00

This is the receipt for the load of scrap in the previous photo.   You can see that it was weighed in and appraised at $225. You can also see the price paid per pound for each metal, on that particular day in December of 2022.

Shop around and compare scrap metal pricing from different scrap yards in your area. This allows you to choose the yard offering the best price for your scrap. Prices can fluctuate, and being aware of the market will help you negotiate better rates.

Establish a relationship with local scrap yards. Regularly selling scrap metal to the same yard can lead to better deals, especially if they see you as a reliable supplier.

Accumulate a substantial load before heading to the scrap yard. Larger loads may result in better negotiation leverage and potentially higher prices per pound.

Copper

Gather copper wires, pipes, and other items. You will need to sort them, however. A nice straight run of copper pipe will be worth some money, but once there is an elbow or a fitting, it will be worth less per pound, because the scrap yard will want to give you the price per pound of the less valuable red brass (more about red brass below). Get a pipe cutter and cut off the fittings and soldered joints.

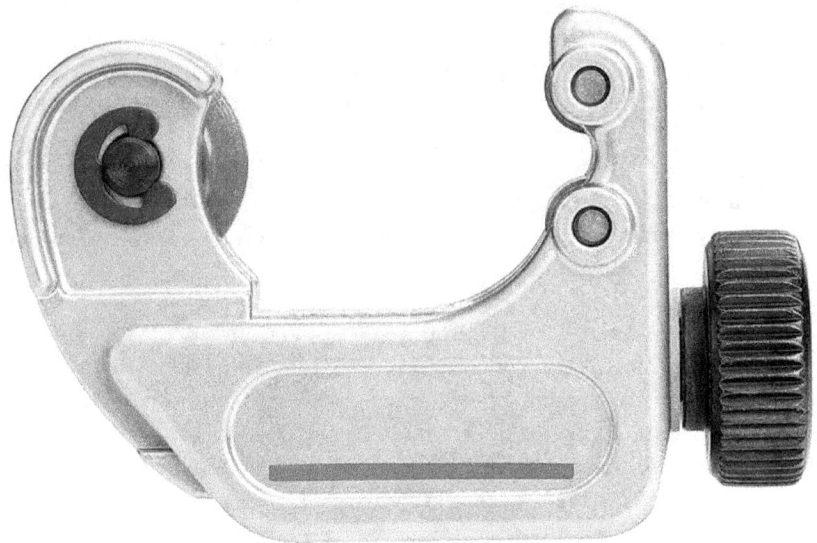

Photo above: an inexpensive pipe cutter.

You can get a pipe cutter in the tool aisle of any nearby hardware store if you don't have one. It will pay for itself a few times over at your first visit to the scrap yard. They come in different sizes. You may eventually want one of each size, but you can get them in the sizes that you need, as you need them. Operating one is easy. Open it up to just a bit larger than the diameter of your copper pipe, and slip it over the pipe. Hand-tighten down the blade with the side screw. Swing it around the pipe a few times, and it will start to move much more freely. Tighten it down a little more, and swing it around the pipe a few more times. Repeat this until you cut through the pipe. Throw the fittings you cut off into your red brass bucket, and now you'll get more money per pound for your copper, because it won't have other metals mixed in with it.

Copper wires, if they are insulated, may be worth less than copper pipe, as the insulation will need to be removed. Keep them in a separate bucket or bin so that you don't get less per pound for your clean copper.

You can find copper wire windings in old electrical motors. You can also find copper in electronics, transformers, appliances, copper cookware, and telecommunications equipment.

Brass: Gather old brass items such as doorknobs, hinges, and old brass lamps. Faucets, valves, some other plumbing fixtures, and in some cases - musical instruments that can't be repaired are made of brass. You can find scrap brass in old keys, spent ammunition casings, candle holders and picture frames.

Aluminum: Gather aluminum items, like old window frames, door frames, old aluminum gutters and downspouts, beach or lawn chairs, and of course, car parts (for example, wheels and radiators).

Older houses may have aluminum siding. (It isn't used as siding any longer, as it is considered a fire trap.) You may find old aluminum wire occasionally. Many household appliances have aluminum radiators in them. Clean and uncontaminated aluminum foil can be collected and recycled. Old or damaged aluminum cookware, including pots, pans, and baking sheets, can be collected for recycling.

If your state does not have a bottle return program, don't forget that you can include aluminum cans in your scrap metal pile. Recycling cans uses 95% LESS energy than creating new ones from raw materials. So recycling cans leads to huge energy savings as well as savings in greenhouse gas emissions. In fact, recycling one aluminum can saves enough energy to recharge almost

20 smartphones. The plastic coating inside a standard can has no impact on the ability of the can to be recycled. It makes up only 1-2 percent of the total mass and is extracted and used as thermal fuel during the recycling process.

Here is a resourceful suggestion for someone with a few basic demolition tools and a pick-up truck: Recycle old above-ground aluminum swimming pools. Once the kids grow up, above ground pools tend to sit in backyards and deteriorate, and they eventually become an eyesore. If you drive by one that looks neglected, you could offer to take it away for free, and then sell it for scrap. Watch the classified ads for these too. Sometimes people will try to sell them, or they will offer to let you take them for free. If someone is trying to sell their old aluminum pool, you could still call them and wish them good luck, and let them know, if it doesn't sell, you'd be willing to come and haul it away for free, as long as you can keep the money you get selling it for scrap. Be careful doing this, however. You may run across an above ground pool that is not aluminum. It could be steel. Look for rust, or better yet, bring a magnet with you to make certain it isn't steel. If you end up scrapping a steel pool, you will get significantly less money, and it may not be worth the effort unless you're getting paid for the demolition.

Iron and Steel

The words iron and steel are often used interchangeably, and they shouldn't be, so let's clear that up first. Iron is literally a basic metal element in the periodic table (Fe). Pure iron is relatively soft and not commonly used for industrial applications. It is used in limited applications, such as in certain types of magnets, as a catalyst in chemical reactions, and in some laboratory equipment. You won't run across much pure iron for scrapping.

Steel is an alloy of iron with carbon and other elements, such as manganese, chromium, nickel, or molybdenum. Steel exhibits a broader range of properties, making it a more versatile material for a wide array of applications in modern industry and construction. Steel is stronger, more durable, and more versatile than pure iron. There are many grades of steel, suited for different purposes.

Steel won't get you nearly as much money by the pound as other more valuable metals. 100 pounds of steel might be worth under $20 at the scrap yard. If you don't have a large area available for you to collect and store steel items until you have enough to make a trip to the scrap yard worth your time, it might be easier to just take steel to a municipal drop off center that will accept it for free.

Stainless Steel

It's important to note that stainless steel comes in different grades, and the value can vary based on the specific alloy composition. High-grade stainless steel with added alloys such as nickel, chromium, or molybdenum tends to be more valuable than basic stainless steel.

Therefore, the price of stainless steel will vary based on factors such as alloy composition, market conditions, and geographical location. The price of stainless steel can range from fifty cents to $1.50 per pound, and these values will fluctuate over time, just like other scrap metals.

Here is a list of stainless steel items that you can be on the lookout for, for scrapping:

Stainless steel kitchen appliances, such as refrigerators, dishwashers, and stoves, often contain valuable stainless steel components.

Stainless steel sinks and faucets are common in kitchens and bathrooms and can be sold as scrap. Old or damaged stainless steel cutlery, pots, pans, and utensils are good candidates for scrap recycling. Stainless steel equipment used in commercial kitchens, including countertops, shelves, and cooking equipment, can be valuable as scrap. Railings, balustrades, and handrails from buildings or structures are often made of high-quality stainless steel.

Certain parts of industrial machinery, especially those exposed to harsh conditions, may be made of stainless steel and can be sold as scrap.

Some automotive parts, such as exhaust systems, fuel tanks, and trim, are made of stainless steel and can be recycled. Stainless steel components are often used in medical equipment, such as tables, trays, and fixtures. Stainless steel components are used in construction, such as beams, columns, and reinforcement bars, and can be sold as scrap when buildings are demolished or renovated. You'll find stainless steel home decor items, including furniture, sculptures, and decorative fixtures.

Red Brass

You may not have heard of this. Red brass scrap, also commonly known as gunmetal, is an alloy that appears red in color. Due to having at least an 80% copper content, red brass is more valuable than yellow brass. Red brass is most often found in use with plumbing fixtures such as valves for faucets, connectors, couplings, and in old water meters. It is also used in the production of jewelry, and some older musical instruments like trumpets and tubas will contain red brass. Spent shell casings, particularly those used in older firearms, can be made from red brass. It is also commonly used in the construction of fire hydrants. Discarded hydrants can be valuable for scrap. Some doorknobs, handles, hinges, and other door hardware may contain red brass.

Brass sprinkler heads used in irrigation systems or fire suppression systems may be made of red brass. Some older automotive radiators may contain red brass components, particularly in the construction of the radiator system.

Lead

Lead is a hazardous material and its use is regulated due to health and environmental concerns. However, there are certain items that may contain lead and can be sold for scrap. It's important to note that dealing with lead requires careful handling and compliance with safety and environmental regulations.

Here are some examples of items that may contain lead and could be sold for scrap:

Lead-acid car batteries: They can be heavy, and if they've been damaged, they can leak acid that can burn your clothes – and you definitely don't want to get it on your skin or in your eyes. The price for car batteries fluctuates, but you can get between $5 - $10 for each one.

In older plumbing systems, lead pipes were used. Replacing these pipes during renovations or repairs can yield scrap lead.

Lead flashing is used in construction to provide a weatherproof barrier. Old or replaced flashing may contain lead.

Some older wheel weights used for balancing tires are made of lead. These can be collected when replaced. As a boy, I collected wheel weights made of lead that I found on the side of the road, that had fallen off passing traffic.

Some older electrical cables or wiring may have lead sheathing. This is less common today due to safety concerns.

Counterweights in certain applications, such as elevators or industrial machinery, may be made of lead. Old windows used lead counterweights. You can collect them when replacement windows get installed.

Used or spent lead shot or bullets can be collected and recycled.

Fishing weights are often made of lead. Fishermen often collect lead to craft their own weights and lures in lead molds. You can find them in old garages and at yard sales. The molds will be worth money to other craftsmen and collectors also.

Precious Metals: Silver, Gold

You're better off taking silver and gold to a jewelry shop, coin shop, or a pawn shop if you have some to sell. In many cases, (but not all) gold and silver will have collectible value, besides its value per pound (or ounce). You can sell it on-line too, but it can be tricky if it comes to a return. Be mindful – that you may be dealing with pure silver and gold, or silver and gold *plating*.

Keep these sources in mind when looking for silver and gold to sell:

Broken or unwanted jewelry, including rings, necklaces, bracelets, and earrings, can be a significant source of scrap silver and gold.

Old or damaged silverware, such as forks, spoons, knives, and serving utensils, often contains silver or are silver plated, and can be sold for scrap. Items with a silver-plated layer, such as trays, dishes, and decorative items, can be sources of scrap silver.

Old or circulated silver coins, particularly those minted before 1965 in the United States (pre-1964 for dimes, quarters, and half dollars), can contain a significant amount of silver.

Gold coins, especially those that are damaged, scratched, or worn, can be collected as scrap gold.

Unused or damaged silver or gold bullion, bars, or rounds can be sold for scrap if they are no longer suitable for investment or collection purposes.

Some electronic devices, especially older ones, may contain components with silver and gold, such as connectors, switches, and circuit boards.

Dental appliances and scrap from dental procedures may contain silver or gold. However, it's crucial to follow proper procedures for handling dental materials.

Older photographic materials, including film negatives and photographic paper, may contain silver compounds.

Antique items and collectibles made of silver or gold, or containing silver or gold components, can be valuable for scrap. Trophies, and decorative items often contain silver or gold.

Artistic materials, such as gold leaf used in gilding, may contain thin layers of gold that can be collected for scrap.

Gold-filled items have a thicker layer of gold than gold-plated items. While they are not solid gold, they can still be collected for scrap.

When collecting scrap gold, it's important to differentiate between solid gold, gold-plated, and gold-filled items. The purity of the gold, typically measured in karats, can also impact its value.

Electronics (or E-Waste)

You can recycle old electronics at specialized e-waste recycling centers. You can recycle old cell phones, computers and printers, television sets, and other electronics. Circuit boards often include valuable metals, such as gold. Extracting the gold yourself, however, requires a lot of time and patience, and it involves the use of toxic chemicals. It's not recommended.

Let's look at the economics of an example. If you were to scrap a large flat screen TV, the gold, aluminum, and zinc you might get out of it would only add up to a couple of dollars in value. This isn't worth the effort for most people, because it would require a lot of time.

Cell phones are a better option, because if they are in working order or can be repaired, you can sell them directly to buyers, rather than scrapping them. They easily fit in a padded envelope. There are places that you can sell them on-line, such as ecoATM.com. You can also donate old cell phones to women's shelters.

Old cameras and photography equipment are another special case. They have become highly collectible. They're small and easy to ship. That makes them another item that's easy to sell on ebay.

Plastic

As an individual, it will be difficult to make money selling plastic. There are buyers out there, but you'll need tons of it. They will be looking for many specific types of plastic.

Do your best to keep plastics from ending up in the ocean or on a south pacific island, and bring them to your municipal recycling center. Recycling plastic film, such as what is used for shopping bags, usually requires a special program that's harder to find.

Speaking of shopping bags, a way to keep them out of the ocean or a land fill, is to avoid using them in the first place, thereby reducing demand. If your neighborhood stores still provide plastic shopping bags, bring your own re-usable bags in. If you keep a few of your own shopping bags in the trunk or glove compartment of your car, you'll always have them handy when you need them.

If you have a lot of plastic plant pots, you might be able to sell them or donate them to a local nursery who can use them again and keep them out of the land fill for at least another season.

It might sound crazy – but you can sell old plastic prescription bottles on-line, on ebay. People use them for storing supplies for arts and crafts, or small parts. Peel the labels off first, and then save them up and sell them in a lot.

Textiles, Clothing, and Shoes

You can sell used clothing to consignment and thrift stores if it's in good shape. There is a market for "vintage" clothing. You can also participate in clothing recycling programs that pay by the pound, but this will obviously require that you collect more. You should be able to find clothing drop-off bins operated by organizations that can deal in the higher volume to make it profitable. Be sure to deposit items that are clean.

Believe it or not, there are places that pay for old shoes. You can sell (or donate) gently used shoes at some thrift and consignment shops. You can also sell them on-line, on sites such as ebay, Poshmark, or Depop.

Concert T-shirts

If you attended concerts in the 70s, 80s, 90s, or 2000s and you have some old concert T-shirts in the bottom of a drawer somewhere, dig them up and look them over. Vintage concert t-shirts can go for big money on ebay and on sites such as Wyco Vintage (wycovintage.com). Wyco has a form you can complete, and they'll give you a quote for your shirts. If they don't fit you anymore, you can cash them in!

Bicycles and Bicycle Parts

Selling Whole Bikes: If a bicycle is in good condition, consider selling it as a complete unit. There are many individuals interested in buying used bikes for restoration or personal use.

You can potentially make money by selling old bicycles and bicycle parts at the scrap yard. There are a few things to keep in mind.

Metal Content: Bicycles are typically made of various metals, including steel and aluminum. The value of the scrap depends on the type of metal and its current market value. Steel will be more commonly found in older or heavier bicycles, while aluminum is often used in lighter and more modern bike frames. Bicycle wheels are often made of aluminum that you can sell for scrap.

Preparation: Some scrap yards may have specific requirements for accepting bicycles. It's a good idea to remove any non-metal components, such as rubber tires and plastic parts, as these may not be accepted or may affect the overall weight and value. You may learn that you'll need to take a bike apart and sort it by metals.

Donation: If your old bicycles are still in usable condition, consider donating them to a local charity or community organization. Some places may accept used bikes, refurbish them, and give them to individuals in need.

Books

You can sell used books to second-hand bookstores, or on-line. Here is a good approach; Research each of your books on ebay. If you have a popular or valuable book in good condition, it will be worth some money to an avid reader or collector. Books that are in good shape, naturally, are worth more. Books that still have their dust jackets, and first editions, are worth more. You may be surprised at some of the books that people find desirable. People collect first editions by famous authors, bibles, travel books, books signed by the author, and there are many special interest categories. You can make thousands of dollars selling books on ebay, and they are fairly easy to ship in a padded envelope – but it needs to be worth your time. Consider that it will take a few minutes to photograph and post a book. (You can choose to auction it, or just outright post it for sale). If a book is not worth at least $10, it might be better to set it aside with others, and take them all to a second-hand bookstore once you have enough to fill up a truck. You might get $40 for a whole truck load, but it's better than dumping them in the land fill. Or – you can try to bring them to a paper / cardboard recycling center, or your municipal recycling drop off.

See appendix A for some additional thoughts about selling books on ebay.

Vinyl Records

Lots of people collect old records. You can sell them on ebay, or at record or specialty stores. If you sell them on-line, you can buy carboard mailers to ship them in – or recycle some of your cardboard flats for shipping.

Another on-line place where you can sell vinyl record collections is Discogs.com. You can set up an account and build your own on-line record store.

CDs, DVDs, and VHS Tapes

You can sell old CDs and DVDs on ebay, or at music and media stores. It's harder to sell VHS tapes, but some people still collect them.

Wood

Selling scrap wood for cash can be a bit challenging, as the market for recycled wood might vary depending on your location. However, here are some potential avenues you can explore:

Some places collect wood pallets and wood construction debris that can be recycled or used for fuel.

Local Lumber Yards or Sawmills: Some lumber yards or sawmills may be interested in purchasing scrap wood for various purposes, such as chipping or recycling. Contact them directly to inquire about their policies and whether they buy scrap wood.

Woodworking Shops or Crafters: Small woodworking shops, artisans, or crafters might be interested in obtaining scrap wood for their projects. Check with local businesses or individuals who work with wood to see if they have a use for your scrap lumber.

Online Marketplaces: Platforms like Craigslist, Facebook Marketplace, or other local online classifieds will allow you to list your scrap wood for sale. Specify its type, quantity, and any relevant details. Be sure to meet in a safe location if selling to individuals. Clean, dry scrap lumber can make nice kindling for folks who burn wood to heat their homes. You can sell it by the truckload.

Construction or Demolition Companies: Construction sites generate a significant amount of scrap wood. Some construction or demolition companies may be willing to purchase or pick up usable scrap wood for recycling or repurposing.

Biomass Energy Facilities: Biomass energy facilities may use wood as a fuel source. While they may not pay much for small quantities, larger facilities might be interested in bulk amounts of scrap wood.

Recycling Centers: Some recycling centers may accept wood for recycling. While they may not always provide cash for small quantities, they can be a responsible option for disposing of wood waste.

Before selling scrap wood, consider the quality and type of wood you have. Clean, untreated wood is generally more valuable. It's also essential to check local regulations and guidelines for the disposal and sale of scrap materials.

Keep in mind that selling scrap wood for cash might not yield significant returns, especially for small quantities. In some cases, you may need to explore options for responsible disposal rather than expecting monetary compensation. Always verify the policies of the buyer, and be cautious when dealing with online transactions to ensure your safety and security.

Your local municipality will likely accept wood construction debris, but you'll have to pay a fee by the pound.

Eyeglasses

There are some organizations that will accept donated eyeglasses that they will refurbish and redistribute. If you have a collectible frame, you might be able to sell it on ebay. There is a market for "vintage" glasses.

Cooking Oil

There are companies that will pay for used cooking oil to make bio fuel. Some offer scheduled pickup. As an individual, your best bet is to bring your used cooking oil to your municipal recycling center.   Restaurants can often find opportunities to sell their used cooking oil, or at least get it picked up without having to pay a disposal fee.

Toys

There is a great market for vintage plastic and metal toys on ebay. People collect them, and you can recycle them and make some money. Don't throw out or recycle an old toy until you look it up. It might be worth your time to post it on-line and wait for a buyer to come along. You can always scrap old metal toys if they don't sell for more on-line.

Printer Cartridges:

As an individual, you may not have many ink cartridges, so you can participate in ink and toner cartridge recycling programs that offer incentives. For example, you can turn in your ink cartridges at Staples and get credit to use towards your office supplies.   Or, visit DoorStepInk.com, and you can get a free shipping label. You can send them your spent ink cartridges, and they will recycle them and make new ink cartridges from them – and they will give you a discount towards the purchase of new cartridges that can be significantly less expensive than what you can expect to pay for ink cartridges at the office supply store.

If you are able to collect empty ink cartridges in bulk, perhaps as a school fundraiser or community project, you can send them to "Planet Green Ink Jets", (www.pginkjets.com), and they will count your cartridges and pay you a per cartridge fee.

PLACES WHERE THERE IS LESS OPPORTUNITY FOR EARNING MONEY

Glass

Many areas have glass recycling programs. Collect glass bottles and jars and bring them to a recycling center. As an individual, you will not have an opportunity to make money recycling glass, as there are too many issues with weight and sorting.

Tires

In most cases you'll need to pay to dispose of tires or to have them recycled. You can make money recycling tire rims at the scrap metal dealer, but they need to be separated from the tire first, which isn't always an easy job if you don't have the special equipment that they have at your local garage or tire shop.

Most municipalities have banned tires from landfills. Tires in a landfill trap water that attracts rodents and mosquitoes. They also consume a lot of space, trap methane emissions and create a fire risk. Tire fires are difficult to extinguish.

One of the leading uses for recycled tires is tire-derived fuel (TDF). TDF is an alternative to fossil fuels and produces 25 percent more energy than coal.

If you are having new tires installed, tire retailers should automatically recycle the old ones for you. If you bring in tires but don't purchase new ones, there's a chance they will be accepted, but likely for a fee. Call and check first.

Paper and Cardboard

You can collect newspapers, magazines, office paper and shredded paper, but unless you live near a paper mill or large consumer of recycled paper products, you'll likely find that as an individual, there's no money in it, because of the high volume that you'll need to collect before you have enough to attract a buyer. It will need to be sorted and kept clean and dry, and this will require a lot of space. You could simply recycle paper through your local municipality because it's the right thing to do.

If you live in, or near Michigan, Pennsylvania, or Tennessee, you may have better luck selling your cardboard than most of us. Try visiting https://unitedcontainer.com/sell-boxes

Appliances

You can get money for old appliances at appliance recycling centers. They can contain valuable scrap metal, but be careful. Some appliances include refrigerant that needs to be properly evacuated so that it does not cause damage to the environment. If you choose to take apart and scrap appliances yourself, you may learn that the time it takes to take them apart makes it not worth it.

Mattresses

When you purchase a new mattress, in many states, a disposal fee for your old mattress is built in. The place where you buy your new mattress may take your old one away for you when they deliver the new one. Ask!

If you're not buying a new one, it can be challenging to make money directly, getting rid of old mattresses. There are a few options for responsible disposal and potential opportunities to recoup some costs..

Scrap Yards: If your mattress has a metal frame or springs, you may be able to take these components to a scrap yard, where you could receive payment for the metal. However, not all scrap yards accept mattresses, and you may need to remove non-metal components.

Mattress Donation: If your mattress is still in good condition, consider donating it to a local charity or organization that accepts used furniture. While this may not result in direct monetary compensation, it can be a way to contribute to your community.

Sell Components: Some people dismantle old mattresses and sell individual components, such as the metal springs or foam, on online platforms or at local markets. You will likely find that this is not a lucrative endeavor, and that it requires effort to disassemble and market the components.

Check with Mattress Retailers: Some mattress retailers or manufacturers may have take-back programs or recycling initiatives. They may offer to pick up your old mattress when delivering a new one, and in some cases, there may be incentives or discounts for participating in these programs.

Before pursuing any of these options, it's crucial to check local regulations and disposal guidelines. Improper disposal of mattresses, such as dumping them illegally, can lead to fines and environmental harm.

Keep in mind that in many cases, recycling or disposing of mattresses may involve a cost rather than a direct financial gain. The emphasis should be on responsible disposal and recycling to minimize environmental impact. Always explore local options, contact recycling facilities, and consider donation as an alternative to landfill disposal.

Concrete and Masonry Products

It may be harder to find a place to get paid for recycling concrete, but most municipalities will at least accept it so that it can be recycled. If you have pavers, bluestone (commonly used for outdoor stairs) cobblestones, flagstone, or even fieldstone, you should be able to sell it using facebook marketplace. As you might expect, you'll get more money for it if it's clean.

Food Scraps

Compost kitchen scraps and make compost. You'll be able to use it in your garden. You can participate in a municipal composting program. This is another place where you'll be able to do the right thing, but as an individual, you're not going to be able to compost enough food scraps to make money.

NOT SURE WHERE TO RECYCLE?

If you're not sure where to bring recycling materials in your area, a great place to start is by visiting the website earth911.com. It has a search tool, where you can enter in the item you'd like to recycle, along with your zip code, and it will tell you where the closest recycling facility for a particular material is. Over time, you will want to develop your own lists. There are also many good articles on the earth911.com website about how to best recycle some special items.

THANK YOU

If you've enjoyed this book, please visit Amazon and give it a positive review. Besides helping us to sell more books, you'll be helping us to encourage others to make some extra money, and reduce the waste on our planet.

If you've got some recycling ideas that you'd like to share, we would be thrilled to include them in future editions of this book. Please share them by e-mailing your suggestion to frank@recycle-for-cash.com .   You'll be cited as a contributor in the next edition.

APPENDIX A

For the purposes of this discussion, let's say you have an old shelf in your basement with some antique books. Nobody in your home is interested in them anymore, and who knows, maybe some of them are worth something. Sure - you might have a copy of Dante's Inferno from the 1800s that has gilt edges and looks like it's never been read, and that might get you over a hundred bucks, but don't be so quick to discount that hardcover from 1967 that seems totally uninteresting and worthless. It could be a first edition by somebody you never heard of, but it could be highly prized by a book collector. Generally, first edition books are the ones that are worth money to collectors or book dealers. You can learn how to identify first editions and then be on the look-out for them.

Book dealers search ebay constantly for items that they know have value. They may have a customer in mind when they purchase something, or they may know that they have a good chance of getting more for your item than they're offering you. You need to make up your mind that you won't let this bother you. You may sell something for a fraction of what it's worth, but you need to remember that this item was sitting on your shelf in the basement collecting dust. Now you've made some cash. Also, when you auction something on ebay, just the opposite may happen. You may sell something that's only worth a few dollars for ten times as much, if you're lucky enough to get two or more bidders fighting over your item. Don't forget, your item may be impossible to obtain in another part of the world. Ebay is available worldwide.

Let's continue with our scenario. You've got this old book. You need to find out what it's worth to help you determine how to set the starting price for your auction. Open up your favorite search engine and type in the author's name and title to see what you come up with.

Look to see if there are other people selling copies of your book on Amazon. See if there are any copies being sold right now on ebay. Do an advanced search on ebay, and look under "sold items" to see what copies of your book have gone for in the past.

Is the copy of the book that you have in good shape? Is it in better or worse shape than the ones you can find being sold on-line? This will impact what you can get for your copy.

Look up your book on Bookfinder: http://www.bookfinder.com/

Keep in mind that some of the sites you may visit are retail price oriented, and you may not be able to get as much as they are asking for your copy of the same book.

If you want your book to sell, try auctioning it at a price that's less than what you've seen it going for on other sites. If you've got time, you can list it for as much or more, and wait for a buyer to come along. Be sure to include some quality photographs of your book. If your book has any defects or shortcomings, be sure to point them out up front so the buyer won't be unpleasantly surprised. Up front honesty is the best policy.

If your auction has been unsuccessful, don't despair. You have prepared everything already, so you could wait a while and put your item up again. Consider lowering your price. Or – there is another option. Switch from an auction to just posting it for sale, at a fixed price of your choice. Then, wait. Sooner or later, if your book is desirable and your price is fair, you'll get an email from ebay notifying you that your book has sold. Wrap it up in bubble wrap and load it into a padded envelope, and send it off to your buyer.

www.ingramcontent.com/pod-product-compliance
Lightning Source LLC
Chambersburg PA
CBHW071200290526
45796CB00007B/88